The Raising of Jairus' Daughter

by Gloria A. Truitt
Illustrated by Susan Morris

Matt. 9:18–19; 23–26
Mark 5:21–24; 35–43
Luke 8:40–42; 49–56
for children

ARCH BOOKS® is a registered trademark of Concordia Publishing House.

Copyright © 1990 Concordia Publishing House
3558 S. Jefferson Avenue, St. Louis, MO 63118-3968
Manufactured in the United States of America

Jesus and His friends had sailed
Across a lake one day.
Jesus helped a troubled man;
Now homeward bound were they.

Many people stood on shore
And waited anxiously.
Soon Jesus would be home again;
Their teacher they would see!

Now, Jairus walked among the crowd.
His face was drawn with worry.
"Will Jesus never come?" he thought,
And whispered, "Oh, please hurry!"

At last when Jesus met the crowd,
The man ran toward Him, crying,
"My little girl who's twelve years old
Is sick . . . I fear she's dying!"

Now, Jairus trusted Jesus, so
Upon his knees he fell,
And begged, "Come lay your hands on her,
For You can make her well!"

First Jesus healed a woman who
Had waited through the day.
Then Jesus left with Jairus and
They hurried on their way.

As they traveled 'long the road,
A man rushed up and said,
"Trouble not the teacher, for
Your daughter now is dead."

When Jairus heard the terrible news
Of which this man had spoken,
He must have wept and felt as if
His heart had surely broken.

Jairus loved his little girl;
To him she was most dear.
Imagine his great hope when Christ
Said, "Jairus, do not fear.

"Have faith in me and just believe
That I can make her well.
Now let's be on our way to where
You and your family dwell."

When they arrived they found a crowd
Of people loudly crying,
"The girl has died! You've come too late!
There is no use in trying!"

Calmly Jesus looked at them,
And asked, "Why are you weeping?
I assure you that she is not dead.
This child is only sleeping."

The people laughed at Jesus, not
Believing what He'd said.
Jesus walked away from them
Up to the young girl's bed.

Jairus and his wife came, too,
And Peter, James, and John.
They knew their friend would help the girl.
His proper time had come.

Jesus took the young girl's hand,
Said, "Little girl, arise!"
Quite suddenly, the child awoke
And opened up her eyes!

Even though they had great faith,
Her parents were amazed!
Right before their eyes this girl
From death to life was raised!

"Get this girl some food to eat,"
Said Jesus with a smile.
Jairus knew his girl was well.
He'd trusted all the while.

Jesus did a miracle.
He gave new life and breath.
He healed the little girl and proved
His power over death.

When we are sad Jesus is sad too. He wants us to tell him we are sad and ask Him to help us; If Jesus could help Jairus by healing his daughter, He can help us when we are sad

DEAR PARENTS:

As you read this story of Jairus' daughter you will have an excellent opportunity to discuss death with your child. Your child may have already experienced the death of a close friend or relative, or may have some questions and fears about dying. What a blessing it is that, because of Christ's redeeming work on the cross and His glorious resurrection, you can explain to your child that death is falling asleep and waking up holding Jesus' hand.

When Jesus told the crowd of mourners around Jairus' house that the child was only asleep, they laughed. This occasion marks the only time recorded in the New Testament that Jesus' words caused people to laugh at Him. People today who do not cling to Jesus' promises may still laugh at the thought that death is sleeping. How ironic that death will end their laughter, while those who have accepted God's free gift of salvation in Jesus will rejoice in their resurrection.

Explain to your child that death can come after sickness and pain. Even Christians will be tempted with doubt and fear as they face death. Then we may cling to Jesus' words to Jairus, "Don't be afraid; just believe" (Mark 5:36 NIV). Jesus' words spoken to Martha as He went to raise His friend Lazarus are spoken also to us, "I am the resurrection and the life. He who believes in me will live, even though he dies; and whoever lives and believes in me will never die" (John 11:25 NIV).

THE EDITOR